A Boy Named George

The True Story of George Washington

Shanon L. Heath

This book is dedicated to my son, George.
May the story of George Washington inspire you always...

Once there was a boy named George. George was a good little boy who always wanted to learn new things. One day, George was looking at a book with his dad. He saw a picture of a tall man in a uniform standing next to a big white horse. George thought this man looked very strong and proud, and he wanted to know more about him.

"Who is *that*?" he asked his dad, with a curious look.

"That is **George Washington,**" his dad replied.

George *Washington*? The little boy thought for a moment. "Hey, my name is George!" he said proudly.

"Yes, it sure is!" the dad said with a smile.

Then the little boy named George thought again for a second. He had heard the name George Washington before, but he still had some questions. "Dad?" he asked, "Wasn't George Washington one of the presidents?"

His dad smiled again and nodded in agreement. "Yes, he was. George Washington was our nation's *first* president," he replied.

"The very *first* president?" the little boy asked, with his eyes wide open. "Wow Dad, George Washington must have been pretty smart!"

"Yes, he sure was," the dad chuckled. "Being president *is* very important, but that's not all he did. You see son, George Washington *was* president, but he did plenty of other things too! He was also a surveyor who used math to explore and map new lands. He was a farmer who used science to develop new crops. As a leader, he inspired others and helped to form a new nation with a brand new government. Still more, he was a husband and a father who cared for his family. Most important of all, George Washington was a citizen and a patriot who believed in his country. When it was all said and done, though, he was simply a good man who cared about others and always tried to do what was right.

"Did you know that when George Washington was a boy, about your age, he got a brand-new hatchet and decided to try it out on one of his father's cherry trees?

"He chopped that tree right down! Then he went out to play on the family's big farm.

"When his father came home, he found his favorite cherry tree chopped to the ground. He asked George, 'Do you know who has chopped down my favorite tree?'

'I cannot tell a lie,' young George Washington said, '*I* chopped down the cherry tree.'

"George's father had been very angry, but now he was proud because George had told the truth. 'George,' he said, 'What you did was wrong, but I am very proud of you for telling me the truth. Because you told the truth, you will not be punished, but you must never do such a thing again.'

"You mean he didn't get in trouble for chopping down his dad's cherry tree?" the son asked.

"No, he didn't because he told his father the truth," explained the dad.

Now the little boy named George was even more curious. George Washington sounded like a pretty neat guy and he wanted to know all about him. "What else did George Washington do?" he asked his dad with excitement.

"Well, son, let's go back to the beginning. George Washington was born on February 22, 1732, in a place called Pope's Creek, Virginia. When he was only three years old, George's father, Augustine Washington, moved his young family to a place called Little Hunting Creek. There the Washingtons owned a small plantation where Augustine built the family a new house along the banks of the wide Potomac River. At their new home, George and his two older brothers, Lawrence and Augustine, Jr., had many adventures. Both of his brothers taught him lots of things like how to hunt and fish, and his dad even showed him how to ride a horse! This was George's favorite thing. Before long, he was riding all over the family farm."

"Wow, it sounds like George Washington got to do a lot of fun stuff when he was growing up, huh, Dad?"

"Yes, he did! George had lots of fun while he was growing up.

"When he was six, his family moved again. This time they settled at a new home along

the Rappahannock River called Ferry Farm. It was called this because of the nearby ferry that people used to cross over the river. His new home at Ferry Farm was smaller than Little Hunting Creek, but it was a place where George and his family could grow crops and make a living."

"Sadly, when George was only eleven years old his father suddenly died. George was very sad! He missed his father very much. By then his two older brothers had grown up and moved away. Now, *he* was the man of the family."

"Did he still get to ride his horse?" the little boy named George asked with concern.

"Yes, yes," his dad assured him. "George still got to ride his horse, and the more he rode,

the better he got. In fact, before long he was the best horseman around. He was so good that his neighbors, the Fairfax family, often invited him to go on fox hunts with them. George had great fun on these hunts and became good friends with the Fairfaxes who owned lots of land in the West. Lord Fairfax, who was the head of the Fairfax family, was very impressed with young George Washington. He liked the boy's strength and energy. He also took notice that George was always polite and respectful and never shied away from a challenge. When George turned seventeen, Lord Fairfax asked him to go on an important expedition with his nephew, Will, to survey and map his vast lands to the west. George loved math, and surveying gave him a

chance to apply all he had learned in the books he had studied in school and at Ferry Farm. George also knew that this kind of expedition would be a great adventure and allow him to explore the untamed wilderness."

Now, the little boy grew concerned. "Were there wild animals in the wilderness?" he asked his dad.

"Yes, and Indians, too, but George wasn't worried. He was too excited about going on such an incredible journey! Along the way,

George and Will became good friends. They saw lots of wild animals including deer, bears, turkeys, and elk, and had many adventures. The two even met friendly Indians and traded goods with them. They told the Indians that they came in peace as they traveled through their lands. Together, George and Will discovered new territory and explored places that had never been seen before. When they returned home, Lord Fairfax and the others were very happy to see them and excited to hear all about the stories of the things they had seen."

"Hey, Dad," said the little boy suddenly. "What about George's older brothers? What happened to them?"

"Well, let's see," said the dad. "Augustine moved back to Pope's Creek to start his own farm while Lawrence joined the British navy and went to fight the Spanish in places like Cuba and

Panama. Then, when he finally returned home, Lawrence moved back to Little Hunting Creek to start his own farm there. Only now, he renamed it *Mount Vernon* in honor of his commander in the navy.

"George loved going to see his brother at Mount Vernon. Lawrence had purchased more land to make the farm bigger and even built a new house right on the edge of the Potomac

River. It was a beautiful place, and George began to visit there more and more as he got older.

"When George was twenty years old, Lawrence became very sick and died. George was very sad that his brother was gone, but Mount Vernon would now belong to him. It became his responsibility to take care of it from then on, and George wanted to make his brother proud. He had always looked up to Lawrence and wanted to be just like him. After Lawrence died, George even volunteered to take his brother's place as a commander in the Virginia Militia."

"What's a militia, Dad?" the little boy asked with a puzzled look.

"The militia was an army formed by everyday citizens to defend themselves against threats like Indians or invaders from other lands," the dad explained.

Now the little boy named George had many *more* questions. "You mean he joined the army? Who did he fight? Did George go back to the wilderness? Was there danger? What about Indians?" he asked all at once

"Whoa, whoa, hold on!" his dad laughed. "One thing at a time! Now, where was I?"

"George joined the army, Dad!" the little boy said anxiously.

"Oh, yes," he continued. "Like I said, George was only twenty years old when he was given a command in the Virginia Militia. Now he was *Major* George Washington. It wasn't long before the governor of Virginia, Robert Dinwiddie, sent him on his first mission. Just like when he was seventeen, George was going back into the wilderness. Only now, he wasn't going to survey and explore. This time he was

going to a place called the Ohio Valley to deliver a message to the French.

"You see son, Virginia was a colony that belonged to England," explained the dad. "In fact, it was the oldest English colony in North America formed all the way back in the 1600s. It was the place where George's great grandfather had settled when he came to America in 1657. Over time, many settlers from Virginia and other places began exploring the lands to the west. These settlers claimed the new territory they discovered for England.

"By the 1750s, however, *French* settlers were moving into this English territory and claiming it for France. George was sent with a very important message from the English government to tell these people to go home. The problem was the French *really* liked this new land and did not want to leave. They were building new settlements and had even made friends with some of the Indians who lived there.

"When George arrived and asked them to go, the French refused." 'We will not leave,' they said. 'This land belongs to France!'

"This was not good news! George knew he had to return home quickly to report what he had found. With this in mind, he took one man with him, and the two returned home as fast as possible! It was a very long and dangerous

journey back to Virginia. Along the way, the two were attacked by Indians and George even fell into an icy river and almost drowned, but finally they made it home. Everyone in Virginia thought young George Washington was a hero and wanted to hear his story.

"It wasn't long before England and France went to war and George was headed back to the frontier wilderness. This time, he went with a great army led by General Edward Braddock. General Braddock had come all the way from England to fight the French, and he asked George to be one his officers. George was very excited and thought this was a great honor, but he also warned the general that the French would not fight fair."

'They will hide in the woods and attack without warning,' George said. 'They will fight like Indians and come from all sides,' he insisted.

'Thank you George,' said Braddock, 'but, I am in charge here and we will do things my way.'

"George knew that the general was wrong, but he obeyed his orders as the army marched in straight lines through the forest. One day soon after this, the French and Indians attacked. They came from all sides and hid behind trees just like George had said. General Braddock was shot and fell off his horse. Many soldiers died, and others began to run. George felt bullets rip through his jacket and whiz by his head, but he was never hit. He even had two horses shot out from under him, but through it all, he stayed with his men."

"Two horses! And bullets right through his coat! Wow, he was lucky!" exclaimed the little

boy. "What happened to the rest of the soldiers, Dad?" he asked quickly.

"George told them to be brave as he settled them down," the dad continued. "Soon, the army reformed and began to move away from the enemy. George had acted very bravely and saved many lives, but the battle was lost. General Braddock soon died from his wounds, as George led the army back to safety. Even though the battle had been a disaster for the British, young George Washington was a hero.

"Back home in Virginia, everyone learned about what he had done. They all heard of how he bravely led the troops to safety and how he had saved many lives. Everyone was very proud of George.

"It wasn't easy, but after years more of fighting, George and the British army finally defeated the French and made them leave.

At last, everyone including *Colonel* George Washington could go home. Finally, there was peace. George was very excited to get back to Mount Vernon. He missed it very much. He was now twenty-six years old and it was time to settle down.

"Soon George met a nice lady named Martha. He liked her very much and it wasn't long before they decided to get married. Martha was a widow who had two children, a girl and a boy, named Patsy and Jackie. Even

though they weren't George's children, he loved them like his own. Many a day he would take

27

Patsy and Jackie with him as he rode across his farm at Mount Vernon. They loved to see all the amazing things along the way. Patsy loved to ride with George on his horse, and Jackie always seemed to find something to get into. George had to keep a close eye on him, but he remembered being a young boy himself and often laughed out loud at the things Jackie did!

"It was a happy time at Mount Vernon. While Martha managed the household and took care of the family, George watched over his farm. He loved conducting agricultural experiments and practiced new farming techniques to make his crops grow bigger and better. Many different things were grown on the eight-thousand-acre farm including wheat, corn, potatoes, buckwheat, oats, and rye, as well as cotton and tobacco. In all, George tested over sixty different types of crops on his land! He

did this to find out which ones would grow best and which ones would make the most money. George also worked very hard to improve the land itself and even figured out new ways to rotate his crops and tried different fertilizers to keep the soil strong.

"Mount Vernon was like a small town. Everything needed on the farm was made right there. Millers refined grains to make flour for bread while gardeners grew fresh bountiful vegetables to feed everyone on the farm. Other craftsmen like blacksmiths, carpenters, painters, and brickmakers produced all the things needed to run the plantation from day

to day. Even clothing and shoes were made right there at Mount Vernon. George also raised many different kinds of livestock, including cows, horses, pigs, sheep, turkeys, ducks, and chickens, as well as mules and oxen that were used to work the land. He even had boats that fished the mighty Potomac River to catch fish to eat. While many of the things produced at Mount Vernon were used on the farm, many of them were also made to sell."

"Who did he sell them to?" asked the little boy with a puzzled look.

"George sold some of his goods to the other colonies," his dad told him. "Like I said, George lived in the colony of Virginia, but there were twelve other English colonies that needed things, too.

"Together, these thirteen colonies traded goods and supplies with each other. This was part of the way that the colonists got the things that they needed to live in America. Many of them, though, like George, also sent some of the things they produced back across the ocean to England. This was the way it had been for all of George's life. The colonists would produce goods and sell them to merchants in England and then buy things back that they needed as well. For many years, this is how it worked and everyone was happy.

"Finally, though, the British king, named George III and Parliament, decided to start charging the American colonists new taxes on some of the things they bought."

Suddenly, the little boy named George had a very confused look on his face. "What's Parliament?" he asked.

"Good question!" his dad replied. "Parliament was the part of the British government that made the laws that all the people had to follow. It was made up of many representatives from all over England. Parliament was also responsible for deciding what taxes the people would pay. The new taxes they created for America were very unpopular and made the colonists angry! They felt the taxes

were unfair, because the colonies in America were not represented in the Parliament in England.

"Many of the colonists complained and refused to buy goods from England until the taxes were taken away. Soon the English merchants were losing money, and they began complaining, too. This created big problems. Before long, all the taxes were taken away. All except one, that is. It was a tax on tea. This made the colonists more upset than ever! You see, son, the colonists in America really liked to drink tea," explained the dad. "It was a part of English culture, but they *really* didn't like *this* tax and thought it was very unfair! Soon, they decided to stop drinking tea altogether and refused to buy it. Ship after ship, full of tea, arrived from England, but the colonists sent them away."

"'We do not want your tea *or* your tax!' they said. Still though, the ships kept coming. Finally, on a cold December night in 1773, men in Boston, Massachusetts, dressed up like Indians and snuck onto a ship in the harbor. The ship was full of tea; and when they got on board, the men found it all and threw it into the water! This became known as the Boston Tea Party.

"Many of the colonists were very proud of what they had done, but their actions had also

made the king of England very angry! Soon he sent British troops to Boston to restore order and take control of the Massachusetts government. This made the people there furious! It wasn't long before leaders in the other colonies became concerned as well. They knew that if the king could take over the government in Boston, he could do the same thing in their colonies, too! Something had to be done and quickly!

"Soon it was decided that delegates from each of the colonies would be sent to a big meeting in the city of Philadelphia called the First Continental Congress. These delegates were men from all thirteen colonies, and George Washington was one of them.

"In Philadelphia, the men talked about all that had happened and what to do next. After a long discussion, they decided that the colonies would stop buying *all* goods from England.

Then, before they went home, plans were made to meet again. By the time the Second Continental Congress met in May of 1775, the colonists were ready for war with England. They knew they would need a strong leader, and they chose George Washington for the job! Now, he would be *General* George Washington, commander in chief of the *Continental Army*. George knew it would be a long and difficult job, but he accepted it. Many of his soldiers were farmers from the countryside. Others were fisherman and shopkeepers. Some were just boys no older than seventeen. Together they formed the army that would fight the British. At first, the Continentals won battles and the colonists were very excited! George's men fought bravely and made him proud.

"Then on July 4, 1776, came the Declaration of Independence. It was a document that

announced to the world that the thirteen
colonies were free from England. They would

now become their own nation called the United States of America. It was a very exciting time, but George knew that winning independence

from England would not be easy. The British army was the best in the world and the American army needed much more training.

"Soon things became harder for the Americans, and they began to lose battle after battle. George worked hard to keep his army together, but many of his soldiers became tired of fighting and decided to go home. By December of 1776, his army was almost gone. The Americans had just lost to the British in New York, and now they were on the run. George knew he had to do something to inspire his troops. He needed to win a victory to give his men hope. But how, he wondered? What could he do that would show his soldiers they could still win this war?

"Then, he had an idea. What if he took his army across the Delaware River and attacked the enemy in New Jersey? You see, George knew that German soldiers being paid to fight for the British were staying there, in the town of Trenton. These hired soldiers were called Hessians and the Americans had fought them once before and lost badly. The Hessians were the best soldiers in all of Europe and were

feared all over the world. George knew it would be very hard to beat them, but he had a plan. He would lead his army across the river on Christmas night and take the enemy by surprise! George knew that no one, not even the Hessians, would expect such a bold move in the dead of winter. It was a very risky plan, but it might be the last chance to save the American army.

"So on the night of December 25, 1776, General George Washington led his entire army

across the Delaware River. It was a very difficult and dangerous crossing and it took all night, but when the Americans finally attacked the Hessians at dawn, they won a great victory. George had saved the army and the cause for freedom! All of his soldiers were very happy but the war was far from over. There would be many more hard times to come. Sometimes it wasn't even the British army that made things hard for

George and his men. Often the weather was the biggest enemy of all!"

"The weather?" asked the little boy named George. "What did the weather do?"

"Well you see, the soldiers of the American army often slept outside in tents," explained the dad. "In the winter time, it became very, very cold. At times, it got so cold that some of the soldiers even froze to death! During the long winter months, both armies would set up camp and rest until spring time. The British always had plenty to eat and warm beds to sleep in, but the Americans often had very little food and sometimes even slept on the cold ground!

"One of the places George's army camped for the winter was called Valley Forge. This was the place where the Americans spent the winter of 1778. Like I said, it was very cold," continued the dad. "George ordered his men to build

cabins so that they would have a warm place to sleep on the cold winter nights. He knew it was his responsibility to take care of his men, so he stayed in a tent just like them until all the cabins were finished."

"Wasn't George cold?" the little boy asked with concern.

"Yes, he was," said the dad, "and wet, too, but George was determined to stay with his men."

"During this time, he wrote many letters to Congress asking for more food and supplies to provide for the army. Now and then, food came, but mostly the men went hungry. Often they had to hunt for their food and sometimes even ate rats and mice just to survive! George was afraid that these men, whom he and the nation were depending on, would simply give up and go home. To his surprise, however, something amazing began to happen! Instead of growing tired and giving up, his men began to truly become an army. Every day they practiced their marching and worked on their skills. They said, 'We're with you, General Washington, no matter what!' "George was proud of his men, and he thanked them. Then he got down on his knees out in the snow and prayed. He thanked God for all he had done and asked him to continue to watch over his army and the United States of America in the days to come.

"For the next six years, George led the army through good times and bad times until the British finally surrendered at a place called Yorktown, Virginia. At last, the United States of America had won its independence! Now, some people wanted to make George a king, but he told them, No! 'We did not fight this war so that George Washington could be king,' he said.

"All he wanted to do was to go home to Mount Vernon and to Martha, and that is what he did. George went back home and became a farmer. Once again, he rode across the beautiful fields of Mount Vernon. Oh, how he loved this place! He had missed it so much during all those long years of fighting.

"Now, he had two grandchildren -- George Washington Park, who was called Wash, and Nelly. Just as he had done so many years before with little Jackie and Patsy, George took Wash and Nelly with him all over his farm. Once again, times were happy at Mount Vernon, and George never wanted to leave!

"Soon, however, his country was calling him back. Leaders of the government were writing a new constitution, and they needed George's help. These leaders knew that starting a brand-new government would be very hard. They also knew that George Washington was the only man who could lead it. Now, they asked *him* to be the first President of the United States.

"George knew it would be a very hard job. Maybe even harder than being General during the war. Maybe the hardest thing he had ever done in his life. He knew the job would be

difficult, but his country needed him and he said yes.

"People everywhere cheered! They were very happy to have **President** George Washington as their leader. Just as George thought, the job was not easy. But as he had always done, he worked very hard and did his best. George served two terms as president, and after eight years, he went home for good in 1797. Once again, the people thanked George Washington for all that he had done for his country. Finally, he could go home to stay.

"George was almost sixty-five years old now, but he still loved to ride his horses and look over his fields. Mount Vernon was as busy as ever. There was always a new project close at hand. Wash and Nelly were growing up, but they still loved to spend time with their grandparents at Mount Vernon. Once again, times were happy for George and Martha and their family.

"Sadly, on December 12, 1799, George became very sick after a long day of riding out in the snow. Two days later, on December 14, he died."

Now, the little boy sat quietly. "George was gone?" he asked softly.

"Yes," said the dad in an easy voice. George was gone, but his spirit continued. George had been a great hero to all Americans, and all over the nation they were very sad. People everywhere remembered all the good things he had done. He was called *the father of his country*, and his friend Patrick Henry said that George was 'First in war, first in peace, and first in the hearts of his countrymen.'

"George Washington was, indeed, a great hero. His spirit lived on then, just as it lives on today in the heart of every American. Across the nation, monuments and statues were built in his honor. Cities and states were given his name.

"In his life, George did many things. He had been a farmer and an explorer, a scientist, and a soldier. He was a son, a husband, and a friend. He was a father and a grandfather. He was a general, a president, and a citizen of his country. He was many things to many people. But before any of that, before the cities and the monuments, before the statues and honors, before all the

brave and heroic things he did, before he was *George Washington*, he was simply a boy. A boy who always did what was right, a boy who grew up to do great things, a boy that became a hero…a boy just like you…a boy named George."

Acknowledgements

Cover illustration by Dick Smolinski, represented by Bookmakers Ltd. any use or reproduction of this image is prohibited without prior written permission by Bookmakers Ltd.

Illustration 1, *George Washington at Valley Forge*, by Tompkin H. Matteson

Illustration 2, *George Washington and the Cherry Tree*, by unknown artist

Illustration 3, *Young George Washington*,
by Dick Smolinski, represented by Bookmakers Ltd. any use or reproduction of this image is prohibited without prior written permission by Bookmakers Ltd.

Illustration 4, *Colonial Farm (The Residence of David Twining, 1787)*, by Edward Hicks

Illustration 5, *Fox Hunting: In Full Stride*,
by Hans Lorenz

Illustration 6, George Washington Surveyor

Illustration 7, West *Front of Mount Vernon*,
by Edward Savage

Illustration 8, *Colonel George Washington*,
by Charles Wilson Peale

Illustration 9, *The Victory of Montcalm's troops at Carillon*, by Henry Alexander Ogden

Illustration 10, *George Washington and Christopher Gist on the Allegheny River*, by Daniel Huntington
Illustration 11, *The Life of George Washington, the Soldier*, by Regnier, imp. Lemercier, Paris

Illustration 12, *Martha Custis*, by John Wollaston

Illustration 13, *Washington as a Farmer at Mount Vernon,* by JB Sterns

Illustration 14, *Mount Vernon, Virginia, Home of George Washington,* by Francis Dukes

Illustration 15, *King George III of England,*
by Johann Zoffany

Illustration 16, *The Destruction of Tea at Boston Harbor,* by Nathaniel Currier

Illustration 17, *General George Washington,*
by Charles Willson Peale
Illustration 18, *Signing of the Declaration of Independence,* by John Trumball

Illustration 19, *Washington Crossing the Delaware,* by Emanuel Leutze

Illustration 20, *The March to Valley Forge,*
by William Trego

Illustration 21, *The Prayer at Valley Forge,*
by Arnold Friberg. For more information on
Arnold Friberg's Artwork please visit
www.fribergfineart.com

Illustration 22, *George Washington and his Family Around Table,* by Perine, George Eward

Illustration 23, *Signing of the Constitution of the United States,* by Howard Chandler Christy
Illustration 24, *President Washington 1795,*
by Gilbert Stuart

Illustration 25, The Washington Monument, Washington D.C.

Illustration 26, Statue of George Washington,
by Jean-Antoine Houdon

Author photo by Kim Jackson Photography

Made in the USA
Lexington, KY
19 December 2011